KOSHER SALT

KOSHER SALT

Contemporary Jewish American Folk
Poetry, Humor, and Philosophic Farfel

MOLLEE KRUGER

A Maryben Book

Kruger, Mollee
Kosher Salt

ISBN-13: 9780991228911
ISBN-10: 099122891X
Library of Congress Control Number: 9780991228911
LCCN Imprint Name: Rockville, Maryland

OTHER BOOKS BY MOLLEE KRUGER

The Swift Seasons, a novel, 2016

The Cobbler's Last: A True Story of Hard Times, War, and the Journey of a Maryland Girl Who Lived Over a Shoe Store, 2010

A Purse of Humorous Verse for the Jewish Woman, 2005

Ladies First: Rhymes and Times of the Presidents' Wives, 1995

Admiral of the Mosquitoes: Columbus and America in Light and Dark Verse, 1990

Daughters of Chutzpah: Humorous Verse on the Jewish Woman, 1983

Yankee Shoes: A Light Verse Saunter Through Our Second Hundred Years, 1975

More Unholy Writ: Jewish Verses and Vices, 1973

Unholy Writ: Jewish Poems for the Non-Neurotic, 1970

TO RUTH

PREFACE

This collection of poetry is published in memory of two courageous journalists who made an enormous difference in my life as a writer. They were responsible for the debut of a weekly column of light verse, "Unholy Writ," appearing from 1967 until 1983 in The Jewish Week, published in Washington, D.C. by Philip Hochstein and edited by his son Joseph.

The column consisted of what writer Calvin Trillin has called "deadline poetry." My weekly output concentrated on Jewish topics often underscored by carefully researched biblical references as well as traditions, holidays, politics, and history. Some readers referred to it as contemporary American Jewish folk lore. An accumulation of the poems developed into a book, *Unholy Writ: Jewish Poems for the Non-Neurotic,* followed by *More Unholy Writ: Jewish Verses and Vices.*

The elder Hochstein, a former senior Newhouse publications editor, introduced the first "Unholy" book with these kind words written nearly five decades ago:

"From the standpoint of the publisher of a weekly newspaper, all poetry we receive (from readers) is superb, and no one's is less superb than another's. This poses a crisis for the publisher that could well prove fatal to his enterprise. A little space simply must be reserved for world news, ads, and even for local news items. How is it possible to discriminate between perfection, without fatal results? Out of a tragic history of hurt feelings, ill-will, and angry cancellations of subscriptions was born a preventive solution—the rule that we publish no poems.

"This rule was meticulously observed by The Jewish Week from its first issue, November 11,1965. Until the issue of July 27, 1967. A few days before, we received a note from Mollee Kruger with an enclosure…about the world reaction to Israel's victory in the Six Day War. It read:

A wall went up in Berlin town, and cleaved with fear that city; The wall-eyed world cried out in shock, "Tear down! Desist! Have pity!" A wall came down in Jerusalem town, and taking another tack, The wall-eyed word cried out in shock, "Monstrous! Put it back!"

"Since that occasion, the poet has sent us many brief and penetrating essays in rhyme, and we have published them all. And no others. But other publications came to envy "Unholy Writ" and we felt it would be an inverse sacrilege to deny her writings more extensive publication. Today, Mollee is the Poet Laureate of the American Jewish press. It's our hope that her rhymed essays will come to number many, many thousands."

Philip Hochstein Washington, D.C., 1970

This year we mark the 50th anniversary of the Six Day War and of the column, "Unholy Writ." The Hochsteins, father and son now deceased, also deserve to be remembered by all of us in the community they served.

M.K.
Rockville, Maryland, 2017

ABOUT THE AUTHOR

Mollee Kruger was a Great Depression baby born in the small rural town of Bel Air, Maryland. The youngest child of Jewish immigrant parents from Lithuania, she published her first poem at the age of twelve in the Bel Air Times, served as editor of her high school paper, and wrote a weekly column, "Teen Topics" for the Harford Gazette. In her senior year she earned a Scholastic magazine award for humorous writing and published light verse in The Woman's Home Companion.

An English major at the University of Maryland, she wrote a weekly column, "Mocking Molecule," for the Diamondback newspaper, served on the Mademoiselle magazine College Board, and became managing editor of the campus humor publication. After graduating, she worked as a copywriter for a Baltimore ad agency until her marriage to Jerome Kruger, an internationally recognized physical chemist. Having moved to the Washington, D.C, area, she freelanced plays and short stories, taught writing courses, and acted in community theater.

A stay-at-home mother of two sons, she wrote and performed in educational television scripts during the 1960s and 70s. Her column "Unholy Writ" appeared in the Anglo-Jewish press. Later she became a writer/editor at the National Bureau of Standards and served on the Executive Board of the National League of American Pen Women. Poems from *Ladies First: Rhymes and Times of the Presidents' Wives* were set to music and developed into a musical production. Now 88, the award-winning writer, honored for her achievement in the arts and humanities, has added to her eclectic body of work with a memoir, *The Cobbler's Last,* essays, short fiction, and a novel, *The Swift Seasons,* published when she turned 87.

CONTENTS

ACKNOWLEDGMENTS

A number of these selected poems have appeared in *Unholy Writ, More Unholy Writ, Yankee Shoes, Admiral of the Mosquitoes,* Maryben Books; *A Purse of Humorous Verse for the Jewish Woman* and *Daughters of Chutzpah,* Biblio Press. Much of the verse originally was written for the syndicated "Unholy Writ" column (1967-1983) in The Jewish Week (Washington) and from 1970-1987 in The Jewish Week (New York) as well as in the Pittsburgh Jewish Chronicle, Kansas City Jewish Chronicle, Dayton Jewish Chronicle, Chicago Sentinel, American-Jewish Outlook, and numerous synagogue and temple newsletters throughout the country. Deepest gratitude is due the late Doris Gold, who recruited the author into the world of feminism via Biblio Press. "America" appeared in Chesapeake magazine, 1993 editors, Vonnie Crist and Marta Knobloch. *Kosher Salt* couldn't have happened without help from Mira, Len, Joe, Dina, Cynthia and Isaac. Thanks to Madeleine Jacobs for keyboarding the manuscript in 2012 while flying high over the Atlantic and Pacific. Ever since 1978 when she hired Kruger for a writer/editor job at the National Bureau of Standards (NIST), Ms. Jacobs continues to be an incandescent source of encouragement and inspiration.

I
OKAY IN AMERICA

JEWISH JOGGERS

How Jewish is jogging?
Unlike the old Greeks,
The Hebrews as runners
Were no silver streaks.

Unless you consider
The times the word "flee"
Appears in the Scriptures
In years B.C.E.

Departing from Egypt,
Or fleeing from Spain,
Or running from Russia,
Our footprints are plain.

Consider our mileage,
The distance we're logging:
We hold the world's record
For marathon jogging.

DOUBLE BAR MITZVAH

By 10:15 the synagogue
Was packed from wall to wall,
Two clans like football fans were primed
To cheer the Torah call.

One boy stood tall, a baritone,
Who caused the girls to rave,
Upon his cheek, a minor cut
Left over from a shave.

The other youth was half his size
Soprano, sweet, serene,
And both were sharp as growing boys
Can be at age thirteen.

Each reading seemed a work of art,
And flawless to the letter,
Each mother cried, each father glowed,
And bragged, "My kid was better."

LOG ON

Our mothers and *bubbes* once laid down the rules,
In no way discretionary,
To quarantine china and delegate tools
That separate meat and dairy.

But now we can learn to keep kosher on line,
Ace ritual balance and checks,
A cyberspace homemaker's blueprint for food,
Kitchen according to specs.

No worry have I that my fishes lack scales,
No animal fat in my crackers,
No gross infiltration of lobster or shrimp:
I agonize over the hackers.

In nightmares I see my computer at risk,
Security weakened, unsafe,
My cyberspace kitchen unshielded from harm,
Defiled by a virus that's *trayf*!

DOG DAYS

"Are dogs un-Jewish?" asks a friend,
"Or has there been a changing trend?"
I searched the bibliotic stacks,
And found her theory full of cracks.

Although one sees in bible classes
Preponderance of sheep and asses,
A servant who is called a hound
In Second Kings, Verse 8, was found.

A living dog, proverbs tell Zion,
Is better than a lifeless lion;
(Though Russian peasants set their dogs
On folk who shunned the meat of hogs.)

The Nazis kept tradition up;
Today Israelis own a pup,
And Yankee Jews are dog-benign,
(But hamsters? There I draw a line.)

THEORY OF RELATIVITY

There's a lady on our street
Freely mixes milk with meat,
Serves up lobster, shrimp, and clam,
Draws the line at baking ham.

There's another few doors down,
Does the kosher bit up brown,
Soaks and salts without a doubt,
Craves cheeseburgers eating out.

'Round the corner several blocks
Lives a girl more orthodox,
Sink for meat, a sink for dairy,
Asks the rabbi, very wary.

But Hasidim from New York
In HER meals won't sink a fork.
There's a moral I am sharing,
Every time you start comparing:

Richer you will find it's true,
Poorer also than are you:
More observant Jews I guess,
You'll discover (also less).

RABBI AKIBA, HELP!

This car pool for Religious School
Is humble and devout;
The children passionately pray
The motor will konk out.

Or may they find a punctured tire,
Or may it come to pass,
That miles away from any pump
We'll be devoid of gas.

One day our radiator cap
Was steaming for some reason,
Shehecheyanu issued forth:
At last they reached this season!

NO FEDERALESE PLEASE

I've sworn I'll never make a bargain
With using bureaucratic jargon,
I'll not be humbled to my knees
By heavy-footed Federalese.

By choice, I have not shown a bent
For *interface* or *implement*.
In fact, I thoroughly despise
Prioritize and *finalize*.

Indeed, the soul within me dies
At mangled words that end in *ize*.
(The only *ize* MY money buys
Is good old-fashioned *circumcise*.)

SUMMER CAMP

Rebecca, the mother of Esau and Jake,
Didn't make lists of the things they must take,
Never put shots in Esau's hairy muscles,
Never got blood counts of Jacob's corpuscles,
Didn't go through all the frenzied gyrations,
Filling out pages of camp applications.
Leah and Rachel, who also were mothers,
Didn't get check-ups for Joseph and brothers,
Never went buying up T-shirts and socks,
Didn't repair broken footlocker locks.
And Eve didn't do it for Cain or for Abel,
I'll wager she never sewed one single label!
For forty years Hebrews kept moving about,
Abandoning Egypt, they tried camping out,
And didn't require so much gear for their tramp
As two little Jewish boys headed for camp.

QUICK CHANGE ARTISTS

*(A magazine article suggests women refresh marriages by greeting husbands at the door
each day in a different costume.)*

The biblical men cherished marriage,
Polygamists down to their toes
With wives for each change of the seasons,
In colors to match a man's clothes.

But now with the harem abolished,
The parts of the sum are the wholes,
A woman must look to quick changes,
Develop a spice shelf of roles.

Deprived of the ancient assistance,
A modern wife undergoes plenty
To keep her man tied to one woman,
But make him believe he has twenty!

IBN GABIROL RETURNS

Solomon Ibn Gabirol, Hebrew poet of medieval Spain, also wrote "Fountain of Life,"
a universal philosophic work, which influenced Christian scholars for centuries. They
claimed it as their own until 1845 when the brilliant Jewish author was acknowledged.

My Catholic friend received a gift,
Stone sculpture for his yard.
"A work of art," he marked with pride,
"Some saintly Moorish bard
Named Solomon, the artist says,
Who copied it in Spain,
A poet of medieval times,
As we can ascertain."
"A bright, unsung philosopher,"
Spoke I, "whose thoughtful pages
Were thought to be a cloistered monk's
And not a Jewish sage's."
My friend, impressed, informed his priest
And parish friends suburban,
Who come on Sundays to admire
"That Arab in the turban."

YARMULKE EXPLOSION

There's a *yarmulke* in my teapot,
And six *yarmulkes* in the den;
There are *yarmulkes* multiplying
In this house of forgetful men.

Scads of *yarmulkes* so extensive
They could circle the whole Equator;
I could service with little hardship
A *yeshiva*, or I could cater.

There are *yarmulkes*, tons of skullcaps,
So it doesn't strike home as treason
That our synagogue in its wisdom
Will be raising the dues next season.

A DUBIOUS OUTLET

Some men have termed Franz Kafka
A pragmatist of myth,
Whose work is much more Jewish
Than scribes named Jones or Smith.

In fact, he called his writing
A praying sort of form,
And flailed away at darkness
As if the pen could warm,

As if the ink could banish
Abandonment or guilt,
But therapeutic writing
Depends on how you're built.

For certain kinds of persons
A journal works, or verse;
For others more neurotic,
It only makes things worse.

WHAT WE HAVE IN COMMON

No one can peer into our face,
And speak about a "Jewish race,"

For Chinese Jews once by degrees
Resembled neighboring Chinese.

And blue-eyed German Jews from Bremen,
Or ink-haired, swarthy ones from Yemen,

Assumed the same genetic code
As non-Jews living down the road.

Then what has kept the Jews unique,
A group apart, historic clique?

A common culture, not our genes?
Monotheistic ways and means?

It's hard to figure out the clues,
And no one knows
(including Jews.)

CRITICS

Reform friends criticize in blocs,
"Your verse is rightwing Orthodox,"
The Orthodox are more lukewarm
And shrug it off as too Reform.

Conservatives tend to impeach,
"If you're so smart, why don't you teach?"
Israelis read in search of clues,
For views of Anglo-Saxon Jews.

While All-Americans insist
The stuff is much too Yiddishist,
The Yiddishists add their percussion,
"Why not write in *Momaloshen?*"

The Hillel kids claim they don't need it,
(And Unitarians don't read it.)

PLOYS OF YIDDISH

Some call it *kugel,*
Some call it *kigel,*
Some call it *pudding* in the sticks,
And some ignore it all
And use a Betty Crocker mix.

Some call it *pitter,*
Some call it *pooter,*
And some eat *butter* with their lox,
Some brand the stuff *cholesterol,*
(Instructed by their docs.)

Some call it *poopik,*
Some call it *pippik,*
Some coyly call it *belly button,*
Some contemplate their *navel,*
And prefer to call it…nutt'n.

LEVITICUS FOR DINNER

They set high standards in the wild
Without consulting Julia Child:
The swine, off nuzzling in the mud,
Has cloven hooves, but chews no cud,
Avoids his likes, and dodge the scabs
Who peddle finless fish and crabs;
Eschew the predatory fowls,
The vultures, falcons, bats, and owls,
But crickets are a sanctioned bunch,
So pack a locust in your lunch
For insects aren't considered dregs
That leap about on jointed legs;
Winged bugs that crawl upon all fours
Should NOT be cooked in soup du jours,
Nor weasel, mouse, nor crocodile,
Though fricasseed or Kosher style,
Nor gecko, hoopoe, popinjay,
(I wouldn't eat them anyway.)

UNDER THE CANOPY

Crowding the canopy,
Ancestors mass,
Watching the bridegroom
Shatter the glass.

Flowers and spectacle
Somehow seem crass
Up to the moment
The groom breaks the glass.

Through Jewish happiness
Sadness must pass,
That's why the bridegroom
Shatters the glass.

Remember the Temple,
Young bridegrooms and spouses:
Jews as a people
Reside in glass houses.

ELECTION ADVICE

(The Talmud mentions the custom of changing a person's name to help him or her recover from illness.)

A name's a mere symbol, the sages report,
Superfluous growth like a bunion or wart.
To alter the name will transform the whole score,
And nullify that which existed before.

Erasing the name will reverse indecision
And cure a campaign separated by fission.
So here's a solution for all nominees
And parties at home and abroad in a squeeze,

For pols whom constituents deem indisposed,
Prescription for winning is herewith enclosed:
There's time yet to grab all the jacks in the game;
If all else is failing, try changing your name.

KNOW-IT-ALLS

The commentator Rashi wrote
To make the Torah less remote,
If puzzled, he would never feign,
But humbly note, "I can't explain."

Then why are politicians glib
With myths and illustrative fib,
Footnoted by self-serving maps
Reorganized to fill the gaps,

Interpreting with dazzling verve,
Each blip, each glitch, each falling curve?
And why, their faces, calm, seraphic,
Do pols stay unperturbed in traffic

And fathom with facility
Those depths which vanquish you and me?
(The reason is the voting throng
Craves answers—even when they're wrong!)

II

KINFOLK AND REMEMBERED FACES

SEVENTH GRADERS

Reluctantly, our two boys dance
A brisk Israeli number,
With Gary Cooper poker face,
Emotionless as lumber.

They cannot meet the scornful eyes
Of peers who stand near smirking,
Their macho friends who have escaped
And call them wimps for working.

Outnumbered by a crush of girls
To whom our boys are grafted,
They didn't mean to volunteer,
Protesting, they were drafted.

Some Jews donate to charities
To tally up the scoring.
They also serve who stand and dance,
Although they find it "boring!"

BAT MITZVAH PORTRAIT

As carefully framed as your costume,
Adroitly arranged as your hair,
Lecho Dodi crowns your perfection
In patterns Judaic and rare.

The intricate slivers of Scripture,
(There's scarcely a phrase that is not,)
Are interlaced, woven with wisdom
To narrate this primary plot:

Youth's frail outward trappings will leave you
As well as the gifts it bestowed,
You'll smile and remember this portrait
A moment somewhere down the road.

BEFORE SMART PHONES

While pondering which way the marriage is heading,
There's no better time for reliving our wedding.
We'll dig out the album of bride, groom, and kin,
And toast the photographer as we begin,
Who painted a saga in film with his lens,
The beans almondine and the roast Cornish hens,
Who blinded our budget with flash after flash,
And rendered his bill for a mountain of cash.
But years flutter by like the shadows of birds,
One picture is equal to thousands of words.
And likewise, photographers knew, despite strictures,
One wedding was equal to thousands of pictures.

BRIDAL SHOWER VIGNETTE

The bride-to-be knelt center stage,
Beneath the twisted streamers,
And opened presents in her lap,
Fish-poachers, china creamers,

A Seder plate, brass candlesticks,
Thick books on making *knishes*.
Her mother, perched upon her right,
Tried not to be officious.

She added to the "oohs" and "ahs,"
The din of women clapping,
But winced each time her daughter tore
The splendid, costly wrapping.

The crumpled trash was smoothed, retrieved
By Mama, with obsession,
Who couldn't bear to see such waste,
(True child of the Depression).

THE FUTURE RABBI

Little Jeffrey learned a prayer,
At nursery school, a Kiddush prayer;
He hurried up and down the stair,
Kept mumbling his Kiddush prayer.

He sang it everywhere he ran,
To drivers of a moving van,
The plumber and the garbage man,
And puzzled tourists from Japan.

His piercing words refused to fade,
They filled the shopping mall arcade,
He sang the dog his serenade,
And thrilled his Mom's Latino maid.

His gentile playmates heard the prayer,
His special Hebrew Kiddush prayer,
But Shabbos with his grandpa there,
Young Jeffery shrugged, "What Kiddush prayer?

AT THE BRIT MILAH

You won't remember who attended,
Never keep our names on file,
Those who carried, those who held you,
Fleeting as Elijah's smile.

You won't recall your mother's anguish,
Father taut as knotted rope,
Generations, dead and living,
Standing here to witness hope.

Years from now when someone mentions
What this covenant attained,
You may grin or change the subject,
Unexpectedly restrained.

Sealed into the flesh forever
That no force can tear asunder
Lives this sign that you're included,
Tiny Jewish Eight-Day-Wonder.

ALBUM TINTYPE

In Gibson Girl shirtwaists
They race up the stair,
The girls from the factory,
"Rats" in their hair;
Past the first balcony
Up to the pit,
Tickets a quarter
On high where they sit.
Today Chancy Olcott,
A voice to revere,
And coming up: Shakespeare,
Prince Hamlet, King Lear.
They dance like a princess
Or grieve like a queen,
Released from the sweatshop
And sewing machine;
Hard candy papers
And old peanut shells
Tossed down with glee
On the heads of the swells,
Red velvet curtain
And ark-lighted stage,
The girls from the factory,
Great-grandmothers Age.

POP'S COUSIN JAKE

When Cousin Jake was sixty
(Or was it sixty-nine?)
He moved down to Miami
To dip in ocean brine.
He found a humble lodging,
A kosher small hotel,
Where oldsters filled the lobby
And waited for the bell.
And all the friendly widows
Would meet each southbound train
In hopes of finding menfolk
With marriage on the brain.
But Jake was too elusive,
("De vimmin von't catch me!")
He took their gifts and dinners
But managed to stay free.
He loved them and he left them,
Each sixtyish coquette,
And twinkled when he told us
"Dey didn't got me yet!"
And when his days were over,
The ladies' eyes were wet,
But Jake somewhere was saying,
"Dey didn't got me yet!"

JUST OFF THE BOAT, 1896

My mother's aunt who came in steerage,
Black wig on her itching head,
Deemed the immigration agent
Inefficient when he said,
"State your last name for the record."
When Aunt Katie chose to yell it,
Answered the perplexed official,
"How's that? Tell me how you spell it!"
"Ignoramus!" roared Aunt Katie,
"No more of this pointless fooling,
You're the one who's educated;
I'm the greenhorn without schooling!"
(It's fortunate the agent heard,
But didn't understand a word.)

FELLOW SHOPPERS

I shop for bagels, kosher meat,
But liquor stores are not my beat
Though sometimes when the Sabbath wine
Runs out, I find myself in line

At check-out points where spirits reign,
And note the shoppers in my lane:
The gourmets bearing foreign tags,
And those who drink from paper bags,

All arms embracing like a boa
The stuff that clobbered Lot and Noah.
They shield their rotgut or Chablis
And vow, amused, while viewing me,

(My Concord grape, my kosher star)
They'd never patronize *my* bar!

III

TALMUDIC TREASURES

STAGES OF LEARNING

(Our rabbis classified four kinds of students. The criteria may also be applied to nations.)

The first is fast to learn things,
And speedy to forget;
The gain wiped out by losses,
Producing only sweat.

The next is slow acquiring,
And lags as well, forgetting.
The plus outstrips the minus,
A consequential netting.

The third's a snail absorbing,
And once the work is done,
Proceeds to disremember,
The hapless, hopeless one.

The fourth absorbs like lightning,
An agile-minded rookie,
And slow to be forgetful,
Remains the smartest cookie.

UNDERFOOT

We found a proverb in a book,
Who knows how old the saying?
We think about it when our nerves
Are on the point of fraying.

"Each nation treads on Israel
As all men tread on dust,"
But dust has staying power while
Metallic objects rust.

What else can scatter and regroup
And penetrate the breeze,
Or aggravate an allergy
With gritty expertise?

As dust outwears the press of steel
And sanctions no successors,
Then so shall Israel endure,
Outlasting its oppressors.

DOWN TO BASICS

Once a heathen came to Shammai
In a teasing, mocking prank,
"Can you teach me your whole Torah
While I'm standing on one shank?

"If you can, I'll join your numbers."
Rabbi Shammai cried, "You clod!"
And he drove him from his presence
With a handy-dandy rod.

Rabbi Hillel, though more gentle,
Took the heathen down a peg,
"Yes, I'll teach you the whole Torah
While you're standing on one leg!

"Do not do to other people
What you don't like done to you;
That's the story briefly stated,
All the rest is residue."

(And while the heathen did a turn,
Wise Hillel added, "Go and learn!")

A MIDRASHIC CHAT

"Please fathom for me, Rabbi,
The reason you surmise
The Lord bestows more wisdom
On those already wise?"
The scholar asked his mentor.
"But why not fools instead,
Why does the Lord ignore them?"
To this his teacher said,
"A rich man and a poor one,
Seek loans, let us pretend,
They come to you to borrow,
To which one would you lend?
Which risk appears the smaller?
Likewise, the Lord will never
Grant wisdom to the foolish,
Who'll waste it, playing clever."

RESOLVED

"The gift of the Sabbath," a pious man said,
"Was not to inspire abstemious dread,
But rather, delight and supreme pleasantry."
"Not so," cried another one, "I disagree!
On Sabbath we pore over books all day long."
A third voice retorted, "You're neither one wrong,
Those folk, who, on weekdays, shun study, of course,
Should Saturday join with the book-learning force,
But those who have studied all week, day and night,
Shall turn to the Sabbath and seek sheer delight."
Their arguments, pondered these centuries later,
Touch modern distractions to which people cater,
So each seventh day, if we taste pleasure's fruits
In place of the synagogue's scholarly routes,
Let each of us honestly answer his buddy,
"I've earned this the old-fashioned way, friend. I study!"

EIGHT DEGREES

The eight degrees of charity?
Maimonides has said:
The first is help to help oneself,
Thus holding up one's head.
The second is to give but not
To know the folks who take,
While these receivers never learn
Who's rendering the break.
The third degree, the giver knows
The persons who accept,
The donor's name in turn becomes
A secret that's well-kept.
The fourth, the pauper knows the hand
Behind the kind donation,
(His benefactor doesn't have
The slightest indication.)
The fifth degree, a contribution
Made before requested.
In number six a person gives
What someone else suggested.
The seventh is a donor granting
Less than asked, but sharing.
The lowest rung? When someone yields
Reluctantly, uncaring.
(One shot the sages didn't call:
The clod who doesn't give at all.)

STAR-STRUCK

A Jewish star-gazer in Talmudic times
Described a strange star "every seventy years."
But lacking PR and a short, catchy name,
He blew it, and Halley's is all that one hears.

Still, keeping tradition, I rose in the dark,
And stood on what suburbs consider a hill,
And locked the binoculars into my grasp
To seek Comet Halley in spite of the chill.

Our ancient astronomer steadied my arm,
Encouraged the quest and admired my gall.
Away in the distance, I spotted a gleam:
A night-light left burning in somebody's hall.

Then, lo! We beheld it, but what did we see?
Celestial dandruff, a galaxy's crumbs,
No luminous legend, yet nevertheless,
I'll know where to find it the next time it comes.

IV

RED BANANAS

AIRBORNE

(A salute to the Israeli company that developed aeroponics, a system which grew plants in computer-controlled troughs, supplying the exposed roots with moisture and nutrients. Covered with Styrofoam lids and using no soil, the plants were described as rooted in thin air.)

Didn't we say that there's something about
The life-giving Israeli air?
So fertile with promise, it grows you a crop,
And makes you a new millionaire.
Imagine, you'll purchase an acre or two,
Protruding from white Styrofoam,
Then wrap it in Near East Reports, wetted down,
And carry your real estate home.
You won't need a tractor or summer or spring
To rack up a desert in bloom,
You'll let archaeologists sift through the sand,
And farm in your nine-by-twelve room.
And when you shall eat of this aerated yield,
You'll grow effervescent in crowds,
And rise above problems of earthly concern,
A *luftmentsh* with head in the clouds.

AMERICAN TOURIST FACES METRIC

A token of our grade school days,
And central to its pleasures:
Blue nickel notebook backed with chart
Of English weights and measures.

Israelis run a metric maze:
Can't read my own thermometer,
And as if Hebrew weren't enough,
What's centigrade? Kilometer?

I best can measure Israel
In these *poetic* meters,
My love in bushes, quarts and pecks
(Not kilograms or liters).

HELL ON WHEELS

Sherut? A kind of taxi cab,
Except it's like a bus.
It grips you in sheer peril like
A padlock or a truss,
And bounds through holy distances
On supernatural wings
Yields Indy speedcar racing thrills
On trampoline-like springs.
You leave Jerusalem and pray
You'll make it in these crates
To Haifa's outskirts, with her signs
Of "Welcome to Our Gates."
And bolting through clogged rush-hour roads,
Arrive a half-hour early,
Convince the only gates you'll see
Are those described as pearly!

THE LANGUAGE OF PEACE

Wrote Emerson, "Say what you will,
You can't say more through language skill
Than what you were and are now still."
So much for language as a tool,
And in the diplomatic school,
A treaty uses words the same;
The terms may tend to hide the game,
But underneath, the fear shows through,
The panic and mistrust accrue
Behind the careful polished phrase:
Though words disguise, emotion stays,
And all your piety and wit
Can't alter enmity a bit.

NEW YEAR RED BANANAS

(Note: Israel has harvested tons of red bananas, a tropical plant from Ecuador brought to the land of milk and honey in the late 20th century. The fruit is said to be tastier than the green variety.)

Israelis have a penchant for
Pursuing every route;
Their citizens burned midnight oil
Developing this fruit.

Bananas tastier than those
One buys in yellow clusters?
We hear they sold like hotcakes, like
Proverbial gang-busters.

Each New Year tries to sweep away
The mire in which we wallow,
At least a sweet banana makes
Things easier to swallow.

Let's pray fresh fruit will give the world
A needed dose of manna,
While Labor wrestles with Likud
To be the top banana.

ISRAEL ROCK

The bus you board from Tel Aviv,
Which stops at every *wadi*,
Collects its local color types,
Ingathers everybody.

The forelocks of yeshiva boys
Swing wide like pendulums,
A sad-eyed Bunche Zweig with beard
Is picking at his gums.

An Arab grande dame, dressed in black,
Toys with her golden cross,
The driver's radio, meanwhile,
Is causing hearing loss.

His captive audience endures
A Hebrew dee-jay's noise,
The same ear-splitting bedlam that
America enjoys.

HEAR, O ISRAEL

(Research shows that some Israeli kindergarten teachers have problems with their vocal chords from shouting, suggesting that more can be done to teach the esthetics of quiet speech.)

A tape recording made at large
In any social crowd,
Will show Israeli citizens
Like conversation loud.

Or when the Knesset meets to act,
It meets the obligation;
The level of the decibel
Befits this talky nation.

The UN proves it to a fault,
They never listen well;
And turn their headphones off for spite,
So Hebrews have to yell.

The voice of Israel grows hoarse,
It rarely has a choice;
To keep alive the Herzl dream,
It has to raise its voice.

VERDANT VISIONS

The Irish love St. Patrick's Day;
Begrudging them is mean-ish,
We hope their holiday goes well,
The wearing of the greenish.

An Ireland torn apart was sad,
A searing convolution,
Israelis know internal strife;
All Jews hate persecution.

My friend, who comes from Ireland's shores,
Says Israel seems kin,
The feisty people in both lands
Punch hard when nerves wear thin.

And when you fly to Tel Aviv,
He says, before you land,
You see the desert wearing green,
A shamrock in the sand.

V
STURDY SYNAGOGUES, ROBUST RABBIS

SLEEP NO MORE

Saturday, the rabbi's sermon
In his quest for timely themes,
Stressed the biblical importance
Of man's supernatural dreams,
Patriarchs inspired by slumber
Joseph, Daniel mining clues;
Several rows before the pulpit
Slumped a Hebrew in a snooze,
And I pondered if the wonder
Of the Scriptures touched his doze,
Would the man awaken wiser
Than before his blest repose?
Afterward, the rabbi's patrons,
Lauded him, but most adoring
Was the praise of that same dreamer
Who had spent the morning snoring!

BEFOREHAND

The question was raised, "On an average day
What do you do before you pray?"
The first one said, "Seek edification,"
Another, "Engage in meditation,"
And one replied when she took her turn,
"A private matter not your concern."
"But only," some said, "if the sky should fall,
Would we ever happen to pray at all."
Then turning it into a kind of joke,
They asked a *nebesh* who rarely spoke,
"So tell us, Moishe, what do you say?
What do you do before you pray?"
"I p-pray," he stammered, "before I start
That wh-whenever I p-pray, it's with all my heart."

END OF SCHOOL DAYS

The battered Hebrew teacher
Throughout the land proclaims
Sweet liberty, like Moses,
To all the tribes she tames.

Shalom to drop-outs, hecklers,
Whose mouths outstrip their brains,
Shalom to *Imma-Abba*,
Who won't take any pains.

"But if I don't, who'll do it?"
They probe the age-old reason,
(And hear themselves agreeing
To teach again next season.)

ADULT EDUCATION

Akiba tended sheep by day
And watched the lonely stars by night,
A forty-year-old shepherd boy,
He couldn't read or write.

His good wife Rachel urged him on,
"For forty years we wandered so,
As slaves to ignorance and fear
An upward path will help us grow."

Akiba learned his *alef-bet*,
And while his neighbors watched in awe,
He rose in stature and became
Their greatest scholar of the Law.

(MORAL:
There's room upon the topmost run
For people not considered young.)

UNMENTIONABLE

Precious little has been writ
Of skullcaps that refuse to fit;
They'll interrupt an earnest quorum
By popping up without decorum.

Small attention has been paid
To yarmulkes so renegade
That they reject (when hair is thin)
A silver clip or bobby pin.

Nothing weighty has been said
Of coverings that quit the head,
Distressing kin, distracting clerics,
And giving teenage kids hysterics.

No agenda has been set
To deal with this potential threat.
(Don't wayward yarmulkes that plummet
Deserve a mention at the summit?)

SAVING GRACES

My mother never threw anything out:
The bakery bags from the bread,
A top from a bottle, a rubber band, string,
"It will all come in handy," she said.

Frayed remnants of cloth, brown cartons, and jars,
The centuries somehow had bred
To waste what is usable counts as a sin,
A maxim that lodged in her head.

Our people never threw anything out,
The writings, the names of our dead,
The exile, the wisdom, the martyrs, the dreams,
("It may all come in handy," they said.)

OF SYNAGOGUES AND TEMPLES

Their melodies may vary some,
But not the faithful flocks that come,
The people, sparkling much the same
As overhead the endless flame.

The *bimah* people shaking hands,
The youths with braces, flashing bands;
The scholars monitor each beat,
A grandpa searches for his seat.

Next week's Bar Mitzvah in the wings,
A tone-deaf voice that, dauntless, sings,
A youthful pair soon man and wife,
The mourners sanctifying life.

Except for dues, perhaps, or name,
The more it changes, it's the same.

VI
AN INWARD PROTOCOL

ANCIENT E.R.A.

Exhibit One: Zelophedad*
Who, praise the Lord, five daughters had,
He died, and here's the point that stabs
His property came up for grabs:
No son. To make the story short,
His daughters took the case to court,
Demanding justice under law,
And what a furor Moses saw
When five young women aimed their sights
And marched demanding equal rights.
Then Moses went before the Lord,
Who told him girls can't be ignored,
They won, despite some dirty looks,
The oldest lawsuit on the books!

*See Numbers 27:1
E.R.A. is the Equal Rights Amendment of modern times.

TABOO

The centaur, never kosher,
Can't chew its cud directly,
Although the hoofs are cloven,
It's structured incorrectly.

The unicorn's not kosher,
Though how can people tell it
When nobody has seen one?
My butcher doesn't sell it.

Nor is the dragon kosher,
By Jews it's unexalted,
A creeping, crawling heartburn,
Unsung, unsoaked, unsalted.

The beasts of myth and legend
Are not for our ingestion,
And when it comes to mermaids,
Don't even ask the question.

GIVING THOUGHTS NO TONGUE

Can letting inward things hang out
Be called a Jewish trait?

To post each nuance of the soul,
To loathe and duly state
Each slur or steely reprimand
Is fashionable of late.

The Psalms petition us to stick
To what we know is true;
The Scriptures praise and emphasize
A circumspectly hue.

Commune, they caution, with your heart,
And painful words keep still,
(The number of us who comply
Is staggeringly nil.)

MODERN PROVERBS

The righteous candidate must be
A lamp unto the rubble,
But one who's crooked in his speech
Will blunder into trouble.

A perpetrated fraud tastes sweet
Till recipes unravel;
And afterward the mouth may chew
An avalanche of gravel.

A soul should not rejoice to see
Its adversary stumble,
The one who's waxing confidant
May wish he played it humble.

(Our Book of Proverbs offers us
In years of our elections
Communiques more accurate
Than CNN projections.)

THE CONVERT

Every section of the Bible
Bears uncompromising truth;
And the Feast of Weeks reminds us
Of a Moab girl named Ruth,

Who has gleaned her hard-earned glory
Through millennia of sheaves
With the loyal scythe and courage
Of a reaper who believes.

For the grandmother of David
Proved that kindness spouts and breeds
Among righteous of all nations
Like a field of barley seeds.

Every born-Jew knows examples
Of the Ruth-like proselyte:
"She's a better Jew than I am!"
Claim admirers (and they're right).

INDIVIDUALISTIC

For no two berries are alike
From blue to straw to boysen,
And what you call your cup of tea
May be another's poison.

And no two pancakes are alike,
When lifted off the griddle,
From raw to medium to done,
And stages in the middle.

And no two marriages are twins,
From grim to bland to jolly,
And no two poets sound alike:
Will Shakespeare isn't Mollee.

And no two Hebrew minds are clones;
The arguments they whittle
May offer more digressions than
"Yes", "No", or "Non-committal."

HANNAH'S BIOLOGICAL CLOCK

(The story of Hannah is found in the 1ˢᵗ book of Samuel, 1-2:10)

Her husband came from fertile seed,
A line of strong begatters,
But somehow she could not conceive;
His fault or hers? What matters
Is lack of tiny feet at home,
The kind that pitter-patters.

Elkanah loved her just the same,
And sought to soothe her weeping,
"I treat you better than ten sons,"
He cried with passions leaping,
But Hannah couldn't eat or drink
As years continued creeping.

She prayed with Eli, local priest,
Who championed her petition;
She promised if a baby came,
He'd fill a holy mission,
And lo, her ovaries contrived
To end her bleak condition.

Contemporary Hannahs tell
New wonder-working stories
Of test tube babies by the batch
Who grow like morning glories,
And mothers thank the Lord for what
He wrought in laboratories.

WHAT'S IT WORTH?

Well, what's a human body worth?
It's risen, like the rent,
Inflated in a decade's span
By manifold percent.

Its calcium, potassium,
Continue escalation,
Its sodium and iron are hit
By runaway inflation.

If Mother Eve were with us now,
She'd be a wealthy madam,
Her calcium is worth a mint,
The ample rib of Adam.

And telling how to get rich quick
From every lecture podium,
Would be the wealthy wife of Lot,
(A profiteer in sodium.)

First Prize Winner, Humor
Virginia Poetry Society

BROTHERLY BREACH

"I dreamed a dream," young Joseph bragged,
"The universe I owned,
The sun and earth bowed down to me,"
("Good grief!") his brothers groaned.

Since Joseph was Pa Jacob's pet,
("My Joe can do no wrong),
The brothers trapped him in a pit.
And sold him for a song.

No doubt they felt a guilty twinge,
And there'd be hell to pay,
But taking all into account,
They did it anyway.

A lesson in this Bible tale:
Pay heed to children's quibblings.,
And never underestimate
The rivalry of siblings.

CIVIL SERVANTS

All civil servants can't be bad,
Before you grind those axes,
Don't trim your nose to spite your face
By slashing at your taxes.

Now Moses formed an agency
Dispensing regulations,
His inter-office memos soon
Became the Hebrew nation's.

And Joseph down in Egypt,
Uncorrupted, without stain,
Once did a fairly decent job
Of handing out some grain.

Isaiah, Jeremiah,
Warned the reapers and the sowers
(They're what is known in Washington,
D.C., as whistle blowers.)

WHICH WAY THE WIND?

*(Note: In Temple times, on the last days of Sukkoth, the Feast of Booths,
a burnt offering predicted the upcoming year's economy, depending
on the direction the wind blew the smoke.)*

Light up the torches, and let the wind blow,
Whither the stock market, folks want to know,
Endless stagflation? A debt limit raise?
Balance of payments in forthcoming days?
Mortgage rates down or perchance go for broke?
Revenues off or sky high with the smoke?
President down to the lowliest yeomen,
Trying to spell out a signal or omen;
Maybe the ancients knew what they were doing,
Measuring which way the smog cloud was spewing;
Should our economists falter or tire,
Let's throw another ox out on the fire,
No need for clamping a wage or price freeze,
Pry off the ceiling and audit that breeze!

OLD SCHOOL TIES

I often tire of what is known
As PR puff and hype,
And all those shallow adjectives
That find themselves in type.

How lucky were the patriarchs,
The prophets and the kings,
The genuine celebrities
Of whom the Bible sings

With eloquently simple strength
And never any need
Of superficial flackery
Embracing words, not deed.

No bubble-headed articles,
No crackling cell phone sound,
Amazing how they made their mark,
And how they're still around!

A GAME OF CHANCE

Experts once said that women weren't
Designed to take a risk,
Few robber baronesses
In those days of Gould and Fisk.

Perhaps we failed to recognize
That Life's a chancy game,
That some you win, and some you lose,
But meanwhile, stake a claim.

Our men took risks in Bible times,
Our Davids and our Sauls,
While women huddled in the tents,
And shuddered at the falls.

Could be we females still recall
How much a risk can cost:
When Eve took chances with the snake,
She gambled, and she lost.

TREATIES

Hasidic sayings hit their mark,
Folk wisdom dressed in black
Presents a common sense approach,
A farmer's almanac.
And so they say the Lord appears
When warring factions cease:
He's present any time we sign
A treaty hatching peace.
Our pundits think the world won't change
The status quo this year;
(Their deity is out of town
He isn't even near.)
A time will come when swords uncross
Though who's predicting when?
The Lord will be the first that day
To hand each side a pen.

RIGHT FIELDERS

*(Note: In Orthodox neighborhoods of Jerusalem, young boys collect pictures of
outstanding rabbis.)*

Jerusalem's yeshiva boys
In earlocks like to shop
For pictures of their holy men
To buy, collect, and swap.

No baseball cards distract their minds,
No bubble gum to chew,
The faces on their trading cards
Depict some righteous Jew.

No Sandy Koufax is their king,
But only pious teachers,
The scholars of their Hall of Fame,
The heroes of their bleachers.

VII
TRIBAL HABITS

DOING TIME

Though I've protested Jewish Time,
The chronic late beginnings,
I'm told that meetings held by blacks
Start halfway through the innings.

They call it Black Time, I'm advised,
Which causes me to wonder
If others like Walloons or Turks
Embrace this social blunder?

Did Mayan tribes have Mayan Time?
Did Caesar's men on marches
Have trouble keeping rendezvous
Beneath the Roman arches?

We Hebrews gave the world a Book
To elevate the masses,
(We also threw in Jewish Time
To wink at hourglasses.)

HOMELESS

Obsolete, perhaps, this query,
Primitive, outworn and droll,
One the Internet can't answer:
Where resides the human soul?

Heathens, long before the Hebrews,
Thought it dwelled in lower beasts;
Others saw the soul as quartered
In the heart, the brain, the priests.

Nations, likewise, have a spirit,
And the Jewish soul abides
In the amity of oneness,
Never rancor that divides.

When a Jew assaults another,
Hatred all that he can give,
Desolate, the soul must wander,
Having lost its place to live.

THE OUTCAST

To try to be funny about Jewish ladies
Will earn me a post in a chamber of Hades,
For those who are touchy or wax analytic
Will damn me as bigoted, anti-Semitic,
And not having taken the Feminist Oath,
To some I'll seem sexist or ageist or both,
A bit overboard on the tired, schmaltzy stuff,
Aggressively passive, not edgy enough.
Too secular, blasphemous, bland, superficial,
And too much the moralist, flinty, judicial,
Too childlike, too cynical, slick, too romantic,
Polemical, maybe, but hardly pedantic,
No flaming obscenities leading the way?
And why let dead Yiddishkeit ruin our day?
Oh, light verse is tricky, and connoisseurs numerous
Declare Open Season on those who write humorous;
(I recognize clearly the dangerous pitfalls,
And gird up my loins to endure kosher spitballs.)

GEMS

These are our folk sayings,
Study them well,
"If they give to you, take,
If they take from you, yell."

These are the guidelines
Our proverbs bequeath:
"You can't hope to chew
With another man's teeth."

This is the wisdom
Our Scriptures recall:
"Display no rejoicing
When enemies fall."

Or, "Peace insincere,"
Say our sages of yore,
"Is better by far
Than a whole-hearted war."

BALANCE OF PAYMENTS

They tell a story ages old,
Or maybe even older:
A *schnorrer* made his beggar's pitch
Before a rich householder.

It was the custom and the right
For paupers to petition
Those Jews the world perceived to be
In better-off condition.

"I haven't got a penny now,"
The landlord said with sorrow,
"But if you'd like to try once more,
Come back again tomorrow."

"If you but knew," the *schnorrer* mourned,
"You never would have said it.
The kingly fortune I have lost
Unwisely giving credit!"

BAR MITZVAH SUIT

Two size fourteens were off the rack,
Two boys were standing back to back,
Two mothers on the spot to boss,
Around one's neck there hung a cross.

We swapped a sigh, a weary grin,
Her boy too plump, and mine too thin,
Her boy was popping at the seams,
No weight on mine, just wistful dreams.

"His confirmation suit," she smiled,
Identically, we clad each child,
And bought their suits as if to stress
How ecumenical is dress.

VOLUNTEERS ON VACATION

Springtime shuffles into summer,
Meetings ended, minutes played,
Still in ghostly cadence, hear them?
Soldiers of the Food Brigade.

Everyone who sliced a bagel,
Set a table, filled a glass,
Sculpted cheese and Nova Scotia,
Aproned, harried, noble mass.

Every hand that baked a brownie,
Ladled punch or offered tea,
All the troops we took for granted,
Marching for a phantom fee.

Till the autumn re-enlistment
Breaks the unofficial fast,
Gone, the chopping, mixing, spreading,
Gone, like heartburns of the past.

DOUBLE STANDARD

When man becomes a widower,
He's begged to come and dine,
The invitations tumble in,
Replacements stand in line.

When widows find they're left alone,
Scant comfort in the cup,
Few cronies whack the bushes hard
To try to fix them up.

When *shul* committees hire a male
As rabbi, unattached,
The congregation seeks en masse
To get the bachelor matched.

But though the single female strives
To keep her flock enriched,
The grim statistics darkly show
Ms. Rabbi stays unhitched.

THE QUEST

Is naked truth beauty? Is beauty bare truth?
How many students can fit in a booth?

How deep the ocean and how high the sky?
What lies ahead in the sweet bye and bye?

When will they ever turn straw into gold?
What is integrity? Whence comes a cold?

Where does the music go after it's played?
Where do our dollars go after they're made?

What is infinity? Yes, what is man?
How many matzo balls make up a can?

VIII
ANOTHER LEAGUE

RX FROM A MASTER

A phantom doctor called on me,
In measured words he spoke,
The ghost said, "I'm Maimonides."
"Is this some sort of joke?"
I answered, knowing doctors don't
Make house calls any more,
But then, retired nine hundred years,
He mightn't know the score.

He scribbled this prescription down
Upon my blanket's borders:
"Mankind," he whispered, "needs good sense.
Please heed this doctor's orders:
Don't ever cast sound reason off
Behind you in a pack,
Because your eyes lie in the front
And not behind your back."

PHYSIOLOGY

Yehuda Halevi, who also wrote verse,
Once cautioned the world populations
That just as the ticker reflects a disease,
The Jews feel the wrongs of the nations
That body disorder and chronic complaint
Beleaguer and hammer the heart,
And zealots who press for a Jewish demise
Are not therapeutically smart.
Today science hallows the organ of life,
That hub of the blood's circulation.
We wish every country were equally sold
On peace and an equal equation,
Though enemies toy with expelling this heart,
Should surgeons perform as desired,
The world's operation might prove a success,
Except that the patient expired.

THE HUMAN TOUCH

Some readers send me roundelays,
And sonnets rich with rhyme;
This desk is piled with lyric odes
They mail me all the time.

Bold cantos, couplets, epic lines,
Nostalgia, wit, and hope,
"Not poetry, but prose run mad,"
(See Alexander Pope.)

They write of rabbis, Bible tales,
The Jewish world off key,
And when they have it versified,
They share their stuff with me.

While technological largesse
Competes to mold our views,
It's good to know those fellow bards
Still wrestle with the Muse.

ANOTHER LEAGUE

In Spain, when the age known as golden
Produced a grape arbor of song,
There lived a poor out-of-place poet,
Convinced that his critics were wrong.

Though lonely and oftentimes bitter,
His mystical medieval pen
Created both hymns to his Maker
And dialogues touching all men.

Bold Solomon Ibn Gabirol,
A poet of reason and rhyme,
Proclaimed that his glorious verses
Were carved on the forehead of Time.

Far down on the list is yours truly,
For modesty, I am a glutton,
And lacking old Solomon's chutzpah,
I'd settle for Time's bellybutton.

STORY OF HER LIFE

A Jewish poet warmed some lines
Within her samovar,
She sent them off to publishers,
And hoped she'd be a star.

But home they galloped like the
Overture of William Tell,
With slips that read, "It's nice but
Poetry is hard to sell."

"Right now," they said, "we publish books
On how to get ahead."
The poet gathered up her rhymes,
"Impossible," she said.

"Me do a self-improvement book,
The kind that reimburses?
If I knew how to get ahead,
Would I be writing verses?"

AUTHOR, AUTHOR!

(Growing evidence indicates that the Five Books of Moses were written by a number of people, not Moses alone.)

A Hebrew professor,
An intrepid fighter,
Insists that our Scriptures
Had more than one writer.

Meanwhile, a computer
Has data on file,
Reporting that Genesis
Stemmed from one style.

New evidence hints of
A mixture of tones,
Some twenty-five authors
From various zones.

I balk at this premise,
Let's talk nitty-gritty:
Since when can such art
Be produced by committee?

HOW QUICKLY THEY FORGET

*(Note: The Dead Sea Scrolls represent only a glimpse of early literature. Many books of
antiquity have been lost and their authors doomed to oblivion.)*

Has anyone here
Followed Jedro the Seer,
Who wrote of his vision of kings?
And when will appear
Works of Iddo the Seer,
Who chronicled similar things?

That prophet named Gad,
Is his work to be had?
If it is, we are given no hint;
Hey, know who could write?
The obscure Shilonite,
Ahijah, who's now out of print.

If agents could find
Ancient books of this kind,
Would they give unknown writers a chance?
Suppose that they did,
If the publishers bid,
To whom would they send the advance?

IX

OUTSIDE LOOKING IN

THE RUINS AT BAIT SHE'AN

I stand on the stage of this
    amphitheater of Bait She'an
       and play to the mob,

       ten thousand eyeless sockets taking note.

My friend stops high on the back row,
    and applauds my chutzpah
       as I milk the silence.

       We are alone.

His voice is wedged somewhere in stone
    between the coming of the next tour
       and the leaving of the last.

       I can hear you perfectly, he calls.

His words come crashing down
    millennia to my feet
       at center stage;
        I doff my white sun visor cap

and make a sweeping bow
       to pure sound and clear heat
       and martyred dust that feeds the Roman frieze
       crumbling nearby.

1984

THE COPTS

In Egypt, where the muddy Nile
Sits squatting on brown legs,
The Copts, a scared minority,
Walk gently as on eggs.

Descendants of the Pharoah's folk,
Who posed for hieroglyphics,
They keep their almond-fashioned eyes
On stay-afloat specifics.

Surrounded by the Moslem mob
And massive reproduction,
The Copts, dependent on good will,
Are leery of destruction.

Despite their story carved in stone,
They keep their profile low,
Somewhat like us, these Christian Copts,
They watch the dice's throw.

CLICHES FROM LONG AGO

A meeting dealt with elephants:
The German gave instruction,
His talk? "A Bibliography
Of Elephant Production."
The Frenchman made the second speech:
"The Elephant in Love."
The Englishman continued with
"Old Jumbo, Hunting Of."
And then a member of our tribe
Arose to give his views:
"The Pluralistic Elephant:
Its Bearing on the Jews."

PARABLE

A hungry pauper, begging hope,
Reaped neither smiles nor sneers;
The people on the icy street
Seemed lodged in distant spheres.

Yet when he slipped and broke a hip,
And in their ambulance he sped,
The guilty town acknowledged him
With sympathy in place of bread.

Our world responds to artless tales
And oversimplified charades;
Confronted by a Holocaust,
Conveniently, it draws the shades.

Though fast to render eulogies,
And sluggish to forestall,
We'd rather mourn the shattered clay
Than keep it from its fall.

FROM FRANCE

In the vineyards of the Loire,
Chambord, Chaumont's river views,
Sleeping Beauty castles doze,
Dream no dream of France's Jews.

From chateaux where barons met,
Kissed their clergy's rings and drained
Blood and gold from Jewish souls,
Only blemished flint remained.

Talmud seized and Jewry burned,
Charge of poisoning the well,
Courtyard roses nod assent,
Jews and lepers bound for hell.

Still, today on Paris streets,
Passing Sabbath-shuttered stores,
Pious men in somber hats
Walk to open *minyan* doors.

A CHAT WITH RAMESES II

(Written after visiting Karnak Temple in Luxor)

They tell me you're the Pharoah
Who refused to let us go,
I stand here at your colonnade
And catch the gusts that blow
The hieroglyphs and callous heights
At Karnak. Is it so
That Rameses, master-builder king,
Was vanquished by us slaves?
The maker of Ramesseum,
Demolished by such knaves?
And now we whisk away the flies
At Karnak. Do the waves
Of silent Hebrews in your halls
Instill a granite fear
That kings don't get a second chance
But Freedom blooms each year?
(A message one can find inscribed
At Karnak.)

VENICE GHETTO

Venetian streets splash mystery,
Brown water laps at history,
A *vaporetto* carries you
To ghetto walls and point of view.
Where once a foundry came to be,
And furnaces discharged debris,
Our people locked themselves from harm
And paid armed guards to sound alarm.

When space allotted seemed too slight,
The houses grew from height to height;
Dense alleys hid themselves in shade
While moneylenders in brocade,
Street hawkers, students, dark-eyed belles
Pinned yellow circles on lapels.

(A tourist comments with a grin,
"It's better outside looking in.")

FAMILY TOTEMS

One summer I found symmetry:
Alaskan totem poles,
Red cedars carved with killer whales
And bear claws black as coals,
Bold images of tribal crests,
Tall crimson thunderbirds,
Commemoration of their dead
In raven's wings, not words.
And someone asked, "Why didn't Jews
Preserve their lives and looks,
Engraving genealogy
On trees instead of books?"
One reason why we transients
Avoided bric-a-brac?
A wooden scrapbook twelve feet high
Is living hell to pack!

THE COUNTRY MILL

A search through faded history books
Of English settlers, royal tracts,
America's green stripling years,
And Anglo-Saxon artifacts,
Revealed to me a Quaker mill,
The ceilings, massive white oak beams,
The wheel and grinders carved from stone,
A trace more Jewish than it seems
For here was ground the *matzoh* flour
In early nineteenth century store
That kept the ancient Hebrew law
And fed the Jews of Baltimore.
Our genealogy assured,
And having staked my simple claim,
I turned the page and read with pride:
Jerusalem, the old mill's name.

THE CATS OF AHUZA

In Haifa the expatriate American,
storms the streets of Ahuza,
impaled on Mount Carmel
high above the porcelain blue teacup harbor
where the Sixth Fleet brews,
anchored like steel Pekoe leaves.

In Ahuza,
the sneeze of a name,
elderly German-Jewish ladies
in foggy-gray suits,
buttoned tight against
the January wind,
complain their way
to the hairdresser.

In Ahuza,
the wingless young American
shudders through the gray inversion,
maimed moth caught
in a cement balcony.

In Ahuza,
she seeks ancestors
past cracked eggshell stone fences
in a neighborhood of tabbies
whose lemon eyes read Hebrew
left to right.

1984

X

SOTTO VOICES

NEW YEAR'S EVE - 1899 AND 1999

You, young girl who are to be my mother,
you sit cross-legged, tailor style,
half hidden by a mound of woolen sleeves
wrought by sweatshop immigrants

I watch you pull gray-white bastings
rip wicked threads
with a hooked silver needle
that bleeds your fingers
into the next century

You'll sleep tonight and will not hear
the bells of days to come
ring out over grimy cobblestone alleys
down gas-illumined streets
that light your way home
through oblivious snow

I, a grandmother now,
stitch these lines to bind us
as we sink together
into ancient featherbeds
from the Old Country:

time and night fetch beginnings
impermanent as chalk lines sketched
by tailors long dead

*1ˢᵗ Prize winner, Catherine Cushman Leach Award, 1994
National League of American Pen Women*

SNOWBLIND

Snow confounds the landscape in the mind,
A Dauchau softens, Vietnam goes white,
The canvas of a massacre unsigned,
Obliterated by a winter rite
That lets us air our linens in the sky;
Snow binds the shattered wildlife on the pike
With tourniquets of crystalline to tie
The wounds that open more than we would like.
Our guilt, commingled with the frozen blood,
And trapped beneath the tundra without trial,
Has no review until the brief of mud
When April passes judgment down the aisle.
With such deceit the snow condones the gun
And lulls us with its virtue, hit and run.

AMERICA

The hindu god
at the convenience store
lifts with a multitude
of sacred hands
the bread and milk
drops them into a
brown paper limbo
smiles enigmatically
and wishes
merry christmas
to the jew
who is still
waiting in line
for the messiah

1st Place, Marion Doyle Poetry Memorial Award, 2008
"for poems of inspiration which are life enriching"
National League of American Pen women Biennial

MARCELLE'S AMULET OF BRUXELLES

This silver tree of life she tilled for me
from inland waterways sustaining art,
hangs on a black-braid ribbon at my throat,
its bright divergence hastening to part
my dense and senseless underbrush of days
that signal nothing flowering of note
except her glow of incandescent hope
that adamantly spreads its roots and stays.

She shaped the vibrant branches when her sight
was quick to see a form when there was none,
and now, though vision cannot guide her hands,
the tree she planted for me has begun
to speculate beneath my autumn skin
and make its own deciduous demands,
renewal and a springtime of intent
that lecture to rigidity within:

light captured by God's metal can deny
the lonely fog that sullies branch and sky;
the Artist's dream sees farther than the eye.

Award-winning Petrarchan Sonnet, 1994
National League of American Pen Women Biennial

SONNET:
TO A LINE IN THE BOOK OF JOB

Read: "Days should speak and multitude of years
show wisdom", so the ancients have decreed
that when a life is counted, bead by bead,
each moment should string neatly into tiers
of righteous size, proportioned by those seers
appraising our intent against our deed,
the gaudy bauble versus noble seed,
bleak talisman assembled by our peers.
But days are unlike words and have no tongue
that translates into mood or banished dream,
abridged Athena lacks a staying power.
Among the spendthrift minutes of the young,
the years are sotto voices in her scheme,
and what seems wisdom changes by the hour.

THE STATUE SPEAKS AGAIN

Give me your tired, your poor (she said)
And never fear abuse,
The new blood feeds my arteries,
I put it to good use.

You brought me your European dregs,
Rejected and despised,
And soon they mainstreamed in my blood,
A land revitalized.

Give me the incandescent core,
That keeps my lamp ignited;
For they belong like all of you
Who came here uninvited.

GLOSSARY AND FOOTNOTES

Page

15   *bubbes —grandmothers; trayf — not kosher*

17   *Hasidim (Chasidim) — pious adherents of Orthodoxy*

18   *Akiba-- early teacher of the Law Sheheheyanu -blessing recited on new occasions and holidays*

19   *circumcise — ritual ceremony performed on newborn boys*

23   *yarmulke — skullcap; yeshiva — rabbinical college or school*

26   *Mamamaloshen — the Yiddish language, mother tongue*

27   *kigel, kugel-potato or noodle pudding; pitter, pooter-butter; poopik, pipik — navel; pronunciation determined by region in Europe where family members originated*

31   *Rashi (1040) — rabbi, author of Scripture commentary*

34   *Lecho Dodi — liturgical song welcoming the Sabbath Bride*

37   *Kiddush — prayer over wine Shabbes (Shabbos) — Sabbath, the Shabbat*

38   *Brith Milah — circumcision ritual ceremony Elijah biblical prophet who attends all circumcisions*

47   *Shammai, Hillel — famed teachers of the rabbinic period*

52   *luftmensh — a dreamer with his head in the Cloud*

57   *wadi — valley or dry gully except in rainy season, an oasis*

62   *nebesh — hapless or innocuous person*

66   *Imma/Abba — mother and father, Hebrew*

64   *alef-bet — Hebrew ABCs*

89   *schnorrer -- begger*

95   *Maimonides — 12th century philosopher, codifier, physician*

103   *Bet She'an — Northern Israeli town, site of ancient ruins*

107   *Minyan — Minyon— quorum of ten Jews needed for prayer*